TV TRIVIA

BEEKMAN HOUSE
New York

CONTENTS

PRIME TIME WESTERNS

Taming the wild west—and the wild characters who lived there—
has always been a major source of TV adventure.
How well do you remember these classic TV westerns?

DOCTOR WHO SPECIALITY QUIZ.....................12

The offbeat adventures of Doctor Who, in all his various personas,
have been a cult favorite for over two decades.
Recall the special magic with this Doctor Who quiz.

WHAT HAPPENED ON THE SOAPS?

Unravel the endless complications that fill the lives
of the characters who people your favorite soaps.
Find out how much you really know about these all-time winners.

TALK SHOW TRIVIA.....................24

Talk shows are designed to do just what the name suggests—
to get people talking. Test your memory of the great moments
and great people in talk show history.

Louis Weber, President
Publications International, Ltd.
3841 West Oakton Street
Skokie, Illinois 60076

Permission is never granted for
commercial purposes.

ISBN: 0-517-48120-0

This edition published by:
Beekman House
Distributed by
Crown Publishers, Inc.
One Park Avenue
New York, New York 10016

Manufactured in the United States
of America
10 9 8 7 6 5 4 3 2 1

Written by: Mark Guncheon,
Frank Lovece, Walter J. Podrazik,
David Strauss, and Fred L. Worth

Cover photos: Movie Still Archives, Personality Photos Inc., Phototeque
Back cover: ABC-TV, Movie Still Archives, Personality Photos Inc., Phototeque

Photo Credits: ABC-TV, pp. 15, 20, 21, 58, 59; CBS-TV, pp. 18, 19; Movie Still Archives, pp. 1, 4, 6, 7, 9, 10, 12, 16,
23, 26, 27, 28, 31, 34, 35, 36, 37, 38, 39, 45, 48, 49, 50, 52, 56, 57, 60, 61, 62, 63, 64; NBC-TV/Herb Ball, pp. 17, 59;
NBC-TV/Gary Null, p. 17; NBC-TV/Ron Tom, p. 17; Personality Photos, Inc., pp. 5, 8, 10, 11, 26, 29, 32, 33, 37, 40, 42,
43, 47, 53, 60; Phototeque, pp. 11, 22, 24, 25, 26, 27, 33, 40, 41, 44, 45, 51, 57, 58, 59, 61, 62

CONTENTS

LAW AND ORDER

From Perry Mason to Columbo to the inhabitants of 77 Sunset Strip, television's detectives line up on the side of law and order. Remember these top cop shows?

FAVORITE SITCOMS

All these well-loved situation comedies get a kick out of some element of the supernatural or bizarre—like a flying nun or an alien from another planet. Meet them here again.

KID STUFF—SATURDAY MORNING HEROES

The shows you watched as a kid provide some of your most cherished TV memories. Get reacquainted with the adventures of some of your Saturday morning super heroes.

TRIVIA ROUNDUP

Your favorite show didn't make it into this book? Maybe you'll find it in this great miscellany of TV trivia. Test your memory with these fascinating quiz questions.

ANSWERS

1 To what state was the wagon train headed?

2 What was the name of the wagon master during the 1957-60 season?

3 Who played him?

4 What was the name of the wagon master during the 1961-65 season?

5 Who played him?

6 What city did the wagon train leave from on the westward trek?

7 Who played the scout, Flint?

4   The original wagon master and the scout, Flint, head the cast of one of television's best remembered westerns.

17 Under what title was *Wagon Train* known in syndication?

18 In 1962 *Wagon Train* switched from NBC and was expanded to 90 minutes on which network?

13 The actress who played that role later starred in her own TV western series. Name her, and the series.

14 What 1950 movie was the inspiration for *Wagon Train*?

19 An actor who played a bit role in the film later starred in his own highly successful TV western series. Name the actor and the series.

8 Who replaced that actor when he left the series?

9 What character did the replacement play?

10 Name the wagon train's cook.

11 Who played him?

12 Chris Hale had a romantic interest on some episodes; what was her name?

15 In the film, who played the role of Travis Blue?

16 What role did Ward Bond play in the movie?

20 A leading cast member died during the run of the *Wagon Train* series. Who was he?

HAVE GUN WILL TRAVEL   (1957-63)

15 The leading character's stunt double became a movie director of the 1970s and '80s. Name him.

16 The leading actor starred in a 1972 TV series in which he once stated that he was Paladin in his youth. Name the series.

17 In 1974, someone won a federal court case in which he claimed that he actually created the character of Paladin back in the 1940s. Who was it?

18 The original choice for the TV role of Paladin had to back out because of an earlier commitment. Name the actor.

19 In 1954 comedian Bob Hope wrote his autobiography with a title similar to that of the show. What was his book called?

1 Who played the show's leading character, the mercenary gunfighter named Paladin?

2 In what city did he live?

3 In what hotel did he live?

4 What was his room number?

5 Name the hotel manager.

6 Who played the manager?

7 What is the wording on the gunfighter's calling card?

8 Name the series' closing theme song.

9 Who sang the closing song?

10 Who composed the series' opening song?

11 Name Paladin's Chinese male servant and the female servant who replaced him.

12 Who played those characters?

13 What type of revolver did Paladin use?

14 What was the name of the first client to whom Paladin sent his business card?

20 Paladin would often quote the likes of Shelley and Keats. True or False?

21 On what TV series did Richard Boone star prior to *Have Gun Will Travel*?

22 Besides his pistol, what other gun did Paladin keep in his belt?

MAVERICK (1957-62)

1 What Hollywood actor made his TV debut playing the role of Bret Maverick?

2 What was the name of Bret Maverick's horse?

3 How did Bret make his living?

4 What was the name of Bret's gambler brother, and who played him?

5 There was a third Maverick brother; name him, and the actor who played him.

6 Gentleman Jack Darby was a partner of Bret on some episodes. Who played Jack?

7 What did the Maverick brothers have pinned on the inside of their coats?

8 Name the Mavericks' gentleman cousin who spoke with a British accent.

9 Who played that character?

10 Who was the only Maverick brother to last the entire run of the series?

11 What was Bret Maverick's date of birth?

12 When *Maverick* was reprised in 1981, what new name was it given?

13 In the new series, what was the name of the town bar that Bret won?

14 Which country singer played Bret's friend Tom Guthrie?

15 Name the 1979 sequel to *Maverick*.

16 Who was the younger cousin of the Maverick brothers?

17 What college did that cousin attend?

18 Who played the cousin?

19 That actor's real-life wife played Nell McGarrahan, his love interest in the 1979 sequel to *Maverick*. Name that actress.

Two dramatic instances of the hard-living, gun-toting Mavericks in action.

1 During what decade did *Rawhide* take place?

2 What was the name of the boss, and who played him?

7 Name Rowdy Yates' horse.

8 Give the cook's full name and his nickname.

9 Name the trail scout and the actor who played him.

14 About how many head of cattle did the team bring to market on each drive?

15 On the set, the actor who played Rowdy Yates earned what nickname because of his long hair?

17 Clint Eastwood became the trail boss on *Rawhide* in 1965. True or False?

18 Who played Simon Blake?

3 Identify the cattle drive's departure and arrival points.

4 Who composed the theme song, and who sang it?

10 That performer recorded a number one hit in 1958. What was it?

11 During the series' 1965-66 season, what character did John Ireland play?

16 Match the actors to the drovers they portrayed:
A. Robert Cabal
B. James Murdock
C. Charles Gray
D. Rock Shahan
E. Steve Raines
F. David Watson

19 What was unusual about that casting?

20 Frankie Laine's theme from *Rawhide* advertises what product?

5 The composers also wrote a famous theme song for a 1952 movie. Name the movie.

6 Who played Rowdy Yates?

12 Who left the series in 1965?

13 *Rawhide*'s leading actor died in 1966 while filming a movie. What was the movie, and how did he die?

1. Jim Quince
2. Hey Soos
3. Ian Cabot
4. Mushy
5. Clay Forrester
6. Joe Scarlett

21 After *Rawhide*, Clint Eastwood went on to appear in a number of Italian westerns. What nickname was given to westerns of that type?

THE WILD, WILD WEST   (1965-70)

12 Name the dwarf who played the character.

13 Name the two horses which the agent kept on his special train.

14 What is the number on the front of the agent's special train?

15 Name the engineer on the three-car train.

16 Who played Dr. Loveless's bodyguard, Voltaire?

17 What was the name of the agent's private railroad car?

18 What was the title of the 1979 TV movie spin-off?

19 What friend of Elvis Presley's served as a stuntman for the star of the series?

20 CBS took *The Wild, Wild West* off the air because the network had promised to reduce violence in its programming. True or False?

1 Name the head government agent on the series.

2 What rank did he hold?

3 Who played him?

4 Under what U.S. President did he serve?

5 Name the two actors who played the President.

6 Who was the head agent's sidekick of many disguises?

7 Who played that character?

8 For a short time the same actor failed to appear on the series because of a heart attack. Who replaced him?

9 What character did the replacement play?

10 This actor also played the sidekick of the series' main character in an earlier series. What was it?

11 What was the name of the agent's 46″ tall archenemy?

The Wild, Wild West's head government agent with his sidekick (above), and in the line of duty (right).

1 What was the name of the Rifleman, and who played him?

2 What was the name of his teenage son, and who played that role?

3 Name the son's horse.

4 Near what town did the Rifleman and his son live?

5 In what state was that town located?

6 What was the name of the bar in that town?

7 Who played Sweeney, the bartender?

8 Name the Rifleman's wife, who died.

9 What type of rifle did the leading character use for protection?

10 How many shots were fired at the opening of the program?

11 Name the Rifleman's marshal friend.

12 What movie veteran played the lawman?

13 What well-known TV actor played a blacksmith?

14 Another actor who appeared as a blacksmith on the series also appeared on commercials for Dodge automobiles. Name him.

17 In the first episode of the series the Rifleman bought a homestead. What was it called?

19 The same actor made an appearance on the next series which starred *The Rifleman*'s star. What was the series?

15 *The Rifleman* began as a spin-off of an episode of another TV series. What was it?

16 Name the proprietor of the general store.

18 In 1962, the actor who played Mark released a record that made the top ten of *Billboard*'s Hot 100. Name the song.

20 This same actor's brother was also an actor who appeared on TV. Name him.

21 On what TV western series did the brother appear?

22 What was his character's name?

23 Before becoming an actor, the star of *The Rifleman* played two professional sports. Name them.

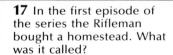
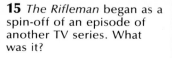

The Rifleman—a hero to his son (above), and (right) a force for the local riffraff to reckon with.   **11**

DOCTOR WHO SPECIAL   DOCTOR WHO   (1963-)

1 Where does the Doctor come from, and how does he travel through time and space?

2 What do the letters TARDIS stand for?

3 What does the TARDIS look like, and why?

4 How old is Doctor Who?

5 Name the six actors who have played the Doctor.

6 How can actors who look so different all play the same character?

7 How many times can the Doctor regenerate?

8 Which Doctor:
A. had a passion for cricket
B. played the recorder
C. drove a yellow roadster
D. wore a long wool scarf

9 Who is the Master?

10 Name the two actors who played the Master.

11 Identify each of the following traveling companions who accompanied the Doctor on adventures:

A. an airline hostess
B. a scientist from Cambridge
C. a warrior from the Sevateem tribe
D. a British journalist

12 Complete this formula, "Reverse the _____ of the _____ _____," and attribute it to the correct Doctor.

13 Which of these is *not* among the Doctor's arch foes?
A. Daleks
B. Ewoks
C. Cybermen
D. the Black Guardian

14 What word would the Daleks use repeatedly in ordering the destruction of their enemies?

15 Who created the Daleks?

16 What metal was deadly to the mechanical Cybermen?

17 Name the Doctor with whom the following companions traveled:

A. Peri Brown
B. Susan Foreman
C. Jo Grant
D. Jamie McCrimmon
E. Harry Sullivan
F. Turlough

18 Which companion regenerated like the Doctor?

19 The six segments to the Key of Time were all disguised. Name the disguises.

20 What was K-9?

21 What was UNIT? And what do the initials stand for?

22 Who was the head of UNIT in Britain?

23 To celebrate 20 years of *Doctor Who* in Britain, *The Five Doctors* special featured all the actors who had played the role up to then. Which two were seen only in *previously filmed* footage?

24 Who said: "Eldrad must live!"?

25 The Doctor's full name is Doctor Who. True or False?

26 Who was Commander Maxil?

27 Who played the Doctor in two theatrical feature films in the mid-1960s?

28 With what handy device could the Doctor open virtually any locked door or jammed device?

The special magic of *Doctor Who*—a delight to sci-fi fans for over two decades.

WHAT HAPPENED ON THE SOAPS? ALL MY CHILDREN (1970-)

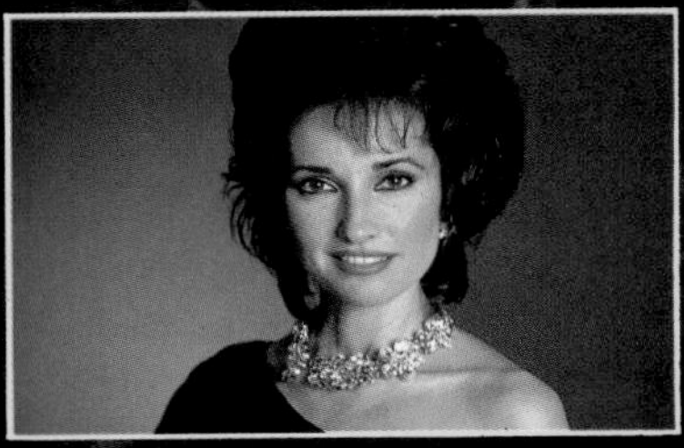

1 What is Erica's complete last name?

2 Name the first person in Pine Valley to die from other than natural causes, and the person who caused the death.

3 Where do Pine Valley's finest ladies have their hair done?
- A. Dial-a-Style
- B. The Glamorama
- C. Kitty's Beauty Boutique
- D. Ken's

4 Langley's long lost daughter, zany Verla Grubbs, was played by Carol Burnett. True or False?

5 How did Jenny die?
- A. drug overdose
- B. suicide
- C. hit by a drunk driver
- D. killed while skiing

6 Who saved Erica when Silver tried to set up Erica for the murder of her lover, Kent?

7 Phoebe Tyler, the lovable lady of Pine Valley, is played by Ruth Warrick, who starred in which classic theatrical film?
- A. *These Are My Children*
- B. *Arsenic and Old Lace*
- C. *Citizen Kane*
- D. *The Gold Rush*

8 Why did Opal leave town for good?

9 In her spare time, actress Elizabeth Lawrence, who portrays Daisy's sensible mother Myra, is a traffic cop. True or False?

10 Match these characters with their occupations:
- A. Sam
- B. Mark
- C. Donna
- D. Marian

1. realtor
2. singer
3. pianist
4. plumber/electrician

11 Who was tried for the murder when Sean killed Sybil?

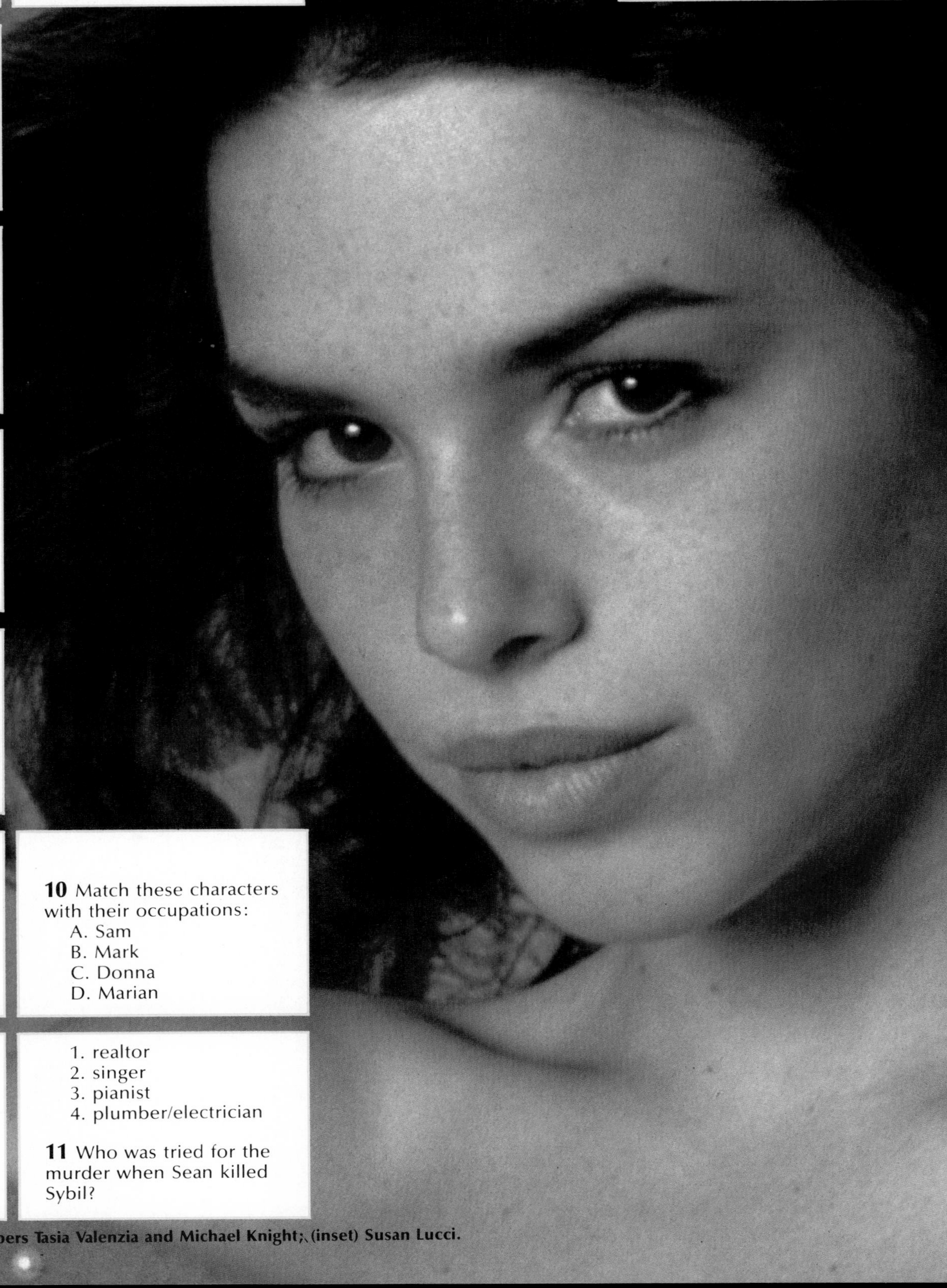

All My Children **cast members Tasia Valenzia and Michael Knight; (inset) Susan Lucci.**

12 Opal was in love with handsome Sam, but he was in love with somebody else. Who was the object of his affections?

14 Who did Charles divorce to marry Mona, Erica's mother?
A. Phoebe
B. Myra
C. Marian
D. Monique

15 Who played Judith Sawyer?

16 Eileen Letchworth as Margo scored a first in soap opera history when she had a surgical operation on camera. What was it?

17 What plot twist was meant to make audiences sympathetic to Erica when she had an abortion?

18 Which character is a diabetic?

19 Ruth Warrick is the only remaining member of the original cast of *All My Children*. True or False?

20 What drug caused Mark's downfall?

21 Lars Bogard was revealed to be which of the following:
A. a burglar
B. a former Nazi
C. the Pine Valley rapist
D. Erica's real father

22 Which came first, *All My Children* or *One Life to Live*?

23 Name the store Myrtle runs.

13 When Phillip was reported missing in action in Vietnam, who did Tara marry?

24 Who introduced Erica at the press conference held for her Erica Kane Cosmetics debut?

15

THE EDGE OF NIGHT   (1956-75)

1 Name Geraldine's TV station?

2 Name her radio station.

6 Preacher was a wandering priest who traveled the streets of Monticello talking to prostitutes. True or False?

7 Who was Calvin's first wife?

12 Name the horror film that Owen Madison made in Monticello.

13 Name Geraldine's two dead sons.

19 Besides acting as Geraldine Saxon, what other role did Lois Kibbee have?

20 What jobs did Sky and Raven pursue after they lost all of their money?

3 Match these well-known TV actors with their *Edge of Night* characters:
  A. Larry Hagman
  B. Tony Roberts
  C. Martin Sheen
  D. Frank Gorshin

14 Raven and Logan's red-haired son is named _____.

15 Why did the criminals go to the Rexford Clinic?

21 Who was Jonah Lockwood, the bearded murderer who tried to kill Laurie?

1. Roy Sanders
2. Smiley Wilson
3. Ed Gibson
4. Lee Pollock

8 What was the name of the religious cult run by Eliot Dorn?

9 Who did Raven really marry when she was first wed to Sky Whitney?

16 In what order was Raven married to the following characters?
  A. Sky
  B. Logan
  C. Kevin
  D. Eliot
  E. Jefferson

22 Though Chris survived a shooting attempt by a masked intruder, she became _____ as a result.

4 Instead of killing Nicole, Pamela Stewart accidentally murdered _____ _____.

5 Name the mind-controlling teen nightclub in Monticello.

10 Who did the fake Sky really kill when he thought he murdered Gunther?

11 How was TV reporter Nicole killed?

17 Who broke Gavin's legs and ended his dancing career?

18 After a long engagement, Mitzi and Cliff finally married. True or False?

23 The fatally ill Denise devised her own death to make it look as though Nicole had killed her. True or False?

24 Name Eliot Dorn's nightclub.

A group study of the cast of *The Edge of Night*, and (inset) Raven (played by Sharon Gabet) and Elliot Dorn (Lee Godart).

DAYS OF OUR LIVES (1965-)

1 Tony's nightclub was called _____.

2 Who bought the nightclub from the millionaire?

6 Name the hospital where the Hortons work.

7 What illness caused Addie's death?

8 Hope had an affair with Roman. True or False?

13 Psychiatrist Marlena treated Fred Barton for his _____ problem.

14 What was Jessica Blake's streetwalker name?

19 Who played Michael Horton?
A. Bobby Eilbacher
B. Alan Decker
C. Wesley Eure
D. all of the above

3 Match the husbands and wives:
A. Tom Horton
B. Doug Williams
C. Roman Brady
D. Mickey Horton

1. Marlena
2. Julie
3. Maggie
4. Alice

20 Actress Elaine Princi played two characters, _____ _____ and _____ _____.

21 Under what name did Linda Anderson return to Salem?

9 What was placed next to the bodies of all the victims of the Salem Slasher?

10 Who was the Salem Slasher?

15 Who played Doug's half brother, Byron Carmichael?

16 What symbol is used to open and close every show?

22 Before she became a doctor, Marie was a nun. True or False?

23 What caused husband and wife Don and Marlena to separate?

4 Why did Neil marry the elderly Phyllis Anderson?

5 When Liz and Neil bought Doug's Place they changed the nightclub's name. What did they call it?

11 Doug's real name is Brent. True or False?

12 Marlena's twin sister was played on the show by actress Deidre Hall's real-life sister, Andrea Hall-Lovell. True or False?

17 Who announces the opening theme sentence every day?

18 Song lyricist Barry Manilow helps choose the music for the soap. True or False?

24 How did Roman die?

25 How does Bo get around town?

26 Name Stefano's symbol.

Four of the characters from *Days of Our Lives*: Tony (top left); Tom (top right); Roman (lower left); Marlena (lower right).

THE YOUNG AND THE RESTLESS (1973-)

1 Name the state and city in which most of the action takes place.

2 Where does Boobsie hang out?

3 Where did creator Bill Bell earn his soap opera writing stripes?

4 What on-camera operation was performed in real life on actress Jeanne Cooper?

5 Young Traci Abbott was once a drug addict. True or False?

6 Match the character with his/her job:
   A. Paul Williams
   B. Ashley Abbott
   C. Danny Romalotti
   D. Julia Newman

   1. model
   2. private detective
   3. rock singer
   4. president of Jabot Cosmetics

7 Before she married Kevin, what did Nikki do for a living?

8 Who died when Kay drove her car off the cliff?

9 What did Victor do to prevent Eve from killing him?

10 What did call girl Gwen do after she pressed charges against her pimp?

11 Name Gina Roma's club.

12 Why did Nikki kill her father?

13 Name Nikki's partner, with whom Kay fell in love.

14 Nikki's husband Kevin was not the father of her baby. Who was?

15 Who fathered Julia's premature baby?

16 When Jack fired Jill in an attempt to end her relationship with his rich father, what did Jill do?

17 When he learned about Julia's affair with Michael Scott, Victor imprisoned Scott in a fallout shelter and tortured him. True or False?

18 To support herself and her son Phillip, Jill worked as a _____.

19 Who saved Traci's life when the despondent teen turned the gas on?

20 To hide from the mob and convince them he was dead, black law student Tyrone assumed what disguise?

21 What is Jazz Jackson's real first name?

22 Name the woman Lauren is always out to get.

23 Why did Brad originally leave Chicago?

24 Who plays Cricket, Jabot's teenage model?

25 To hide her disfigurement, which had been caused in a fire, Vanessa wore a _____.

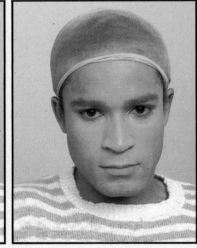

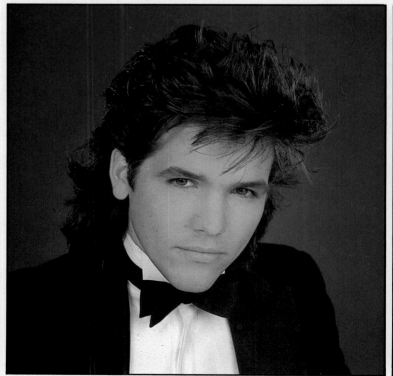

GENERAL HOSPITAL (1963-)

1 Who portrayed Mickey Miller on *General Hospital*?

2 How old was Genie Francis when she first played Laura?

3 Anthony Geary did many of his passionate under-the-covers bed scenes while he was naked. True or False?

4 Who killed Dr. Lesley Webber?

5 Name the star of *Get Smart* who played Wyatt Chamberlain.

6 According to legend, the first thing actor Anthony Geary told producer Gloria Monty was, "I hate soap operas." True or False?

7 When Bobbie Spencer acted viciously toward her rival, Laura Vining, actress Jackie Zeman received death threats. True or False?

8 Before his rape scene with Laura in *General Hospital*, what part had Anthony Geary played on *The Young and the Restless*?

9 The wedding of Luke and Laura was watched by more than half of the country's daytime viewers. True or False?

10 Who killed wife-beater D. L. Brock?

11 Which top movie actress played Helena Cassadine?

12 Where did Nurse Lucille "Sarge" March go after her stint at General?

13 What lie did Audrey tell Tom about Tommy's birth, and why did she lie?

14 How did Mikos die?

15 Name the Cassadine yacht.

16 Who did the secret agent Grant Putnam work for?

17 Match the actors with the characters:

A. John Beradino
B. Roy Thinnes
C. James Sikking
D. Sammy Davis, Jr.

1. Eddie Phillips
2. Dr. Phil Brewer
3. Dr. Steve Hardy
4. Dr. Jim Hobart

18 Bobbie tried to make Dr. Noah Drake fall in love with her by pretending she was:
A. unhappy over a broken love affair
B. blind
C. pregnant
D. a victim of abuse

19 The diner run by Rose and then Ruby near the waterfront was called:
A. Rosie's
B. Nellie's
C. Ruby's
D. Kelly's

20 What fatal disease almost wiped out the staff of General Hospital?

21 Why did Mai Lin leave town?

22 What device did Dr. Hector Jerrold invent that cost him his life at the hands of Grant, Gregory, and Natalie?

23 Name the country David Gray planned to overthrow.

THE SOAPS
THE SECRET STORM   (1954-74)

13 Kip was sent to jail for accidentally killing _____.

14 Where did Amy go to college?

15 How did Belle's daughter Robin die?

16 Dan Kincaid was running a drug ring and seeking election to political office at the same time. What appointment did he want?

17 Was Dan elected to office?

18 Amy had herself artificially impregnated because she had told her impotent husband that she was pregnant by him. True or False?

19 What *Secret Storm* resident always wanted the latest racing cars?

20 Name Peter's three wives.

21 How did Peter die?

1 Name the town in which *The Secret Storm* is set.

2 When the show premiered in 1954, was the opening tone happy or sad?

3 Why was Jerry Ames sent to a reform school?

4 Who did Lauri think haunted her house?

5 What was psychotic Eric's claim to fame?

6 How did Eric die?

7 Mark left the priesthood, married Lauri, and lived happily ever after. True or False?

8 What did professor Paul Britton teach?

9 What musical instrument did Lauri play?

10 When Alan married Susan, he gave up _____ to become an investment banker.

11 After her affair with Paul, Amy suffered a miscarriage. True or False?

12 Where had Jane's long-lost husband Bruce Edwards been?

22 What caused Kevin's paralysis?

23 Did he ever walk again?

24 Why did Belle leave Woodbridge?

The Secret Storm: A cast study (top). Lower right: Characters Susan Ames and Frank Carver.

DARK SHADOWS (1966-71)

1 Which doctor fell in love with Barnabas?

2 In what town was *Dark Shadows* set?

3 Where were exteriors actually shot?

10 Jackie Onassis was a big fan of this off-beat soap. True or False?

11 Actor Jonathan Frid used a special prop for public appearances. What was it?

14 What character did Christopher Pennock play?
A. Cyrus Longworth
B. Jeb Hawks
C. Gabriel Collins
D. all of the above

18 Why didn't Barnabas want to be a vampire any longer?

19 Name the two theatrical movies that were spin-offs of the show.

4 Name the star of today's *All My Children* who played Roger Collins.

5 How many characters did actor Thayer David play during the run of the show?

6 Kate Jackson once starred on *Dark Shadows*. True or False?

7 How was Barnabas different from all of the other characters on the show?

8 *Dark Shadows* was scheduled in a late-afternoon time slot because the network wanted to attract the after-school teenage audience. True or False?

12 Barnabas Collins was Flora Collins':
A. brother
B. husband
C. cousin
D. father

15 Who was the subject of the painting above the living room fireplace?

16 Name the modern film actress who thrilled viewers as Amanda Harris and Olivia Corey.

20 What was actor Jonathan Frid's biggest problem during the taping of the soap?

21 Why was Victoria Winters sent to the Collins' house?

9 Producer Dan Curtis got the idea for *Dark Shadows* from:
A. a dream
B. a story he'd been told as a child
C. a Gothic novel
D. Bram Stoker's *Dracula*

13 Before *Dark Shadows*, how many daytime soaps had veteran screen actress Joan Bennett starred in?

17 *Dark Shadows* was a big hit again when it was recently reintroduced to national audiences through syndication. True or False?

22 What characters did Robert Rodan and Marie Wallace play?

23 What kind of acting was Jonathan Frid noted for before he appeared in *Dark Shadows*?

Why didn't this leading character on *Dark Shadows* want to be a vampire any longer? Check the quiz to find out.

TALK SHOW TRIVIA

11 What is Skitch Henderson's real first name?

13 The first guest on *Donahue* was Madalyn Murray O'Hair. True or False?

7 What is Doc Severinsen's real first name?

8 Joe Pyne was a Navy frogman. True or False?

9 What is Steve Allen's theme song that he wrote himself?

10 How was Johnny Carson billed when he was a teenage magician?

12 The men on the street on Steve Allen's *Tonight Show* were Louis Nye, Don Knotts, and _____.

14 In what year did Jack Paar take over as host of *The Tonight Show*?
A. 1954
B. 1957
C. 1958
D. 1960

TALK SHOW TRIVIA

15 In which branch of the armed services did Ed McMahon serve?
  A. Army
  B. Navy
  C. Marines

18 Who is the current permanent substitute hostess for *The Tonight Show*?

19 In what state was Johnny Carson born?

16 Who was the announcer when Steve Allen hosted *The Tonight Show*?

17 Who walked off the program when a joke was censored?

20 What show on ABC was Carson hosting immediately before taking over *The Tonight Show*?

21 Who led the orchestra while Jack Parr was host of *The Tonight Show*?

22 Who composed "Johnny's Theme"?

23 Who is married to actress Carrie Nye?

24 Cary Grant has never appeared as a guest on *The Tonight Show*. True or False?

LAW AND ORDER   DRAGNET   (1951-59, 1967-70)

10 Jack Webb was producer, director, star, and sole writer for *Dragnet*. True or False?

11 What was Jack Webb's production company called?

12 How was the logo run at the end of each episode?

13 When *Dragnet* returned in 1967, the narrator had a new partner. Name him.

19 What talk show featured Jack Webb in a parody of his own deadpan delivery, discussing "clean copper clappers copped from the closet by kleptomaniac Claude Cooper from Cleveland"?

5 Who played that character?

6 Complete this phrase: "Just the _____, _____."

14 Who played that character?

15 There was a slight change in the title for the new run of the series. How was it changed?

20 The title of the 1954 theatrical feature film version of the *Dragnet* series was also *Dragnet*. True or False?

1 The *Dragnet* episodes were drawn from actual case histories—from which city's police files?

2 Who narrated each story?

7 What was number 714?

8 *Dragnet* became the first series to use color regularly. True or False?

16 During its first 12 months on the air, *Dragnet* ran every other Thursday. Name the police show that it was alternated with.

21 Was Sgt. Friday ever promoted?

22 At the end of each episode, what information were viewers given?

3 What rank did the narrator hold on the police force?

4 Who was the narrator's partner throughout most of the 1950s?

9 On each episode of *Dragnet*, viewers were assured that the story they had just seen was true, with only the names changed in order to "_____ the _____."

17 In 1953, the *Dragnet* theme became an international hit as recorded by which artist?

18 Who released the *Dragnet* parody record, "St. George and the Dragonet"?

23 What crime series did Jack Webb produce in 1968 that went on to last seven years?

77 SUNSET STRIP (1958-64)

1 Who had offices located at 77 Sunset Strip?

2 Who played those characters?

6 Roscoe, their local contact/tout, had a weakness for what form of gambling:
A. poker
B. dog racing
C. horse racing
D. blackjack

10 Did he ever get his wish?

11 When Kookie moved on, who became the new regular parking lot attendant?

14 In the pilot film for the series, Edd Byrnes played a different role—he was a villain. True or False?

3 They were different from traditional hard-boiled "gumshoe" TV detectives in that they were witty, sophisticated, and at home anywhere in the world. True or False?

7 Name the restaurant located next to 77 Sunset Strip:
A. Carlo's
B. Dino's
C. Rollo's
D. Gino's

12 What was the most distinctive feature of the 77 Sunset Strip theme song?

15 During a contract dispute with Edd Byrnes, Warner Bros. brought in Troy Donahue. When Byrnes returned, Donahue went on to his own detective series. What was it called?

4 Name their receptionist.

5 She was played by Jacqueline Beer, who was:
A. a former Olympic gymnast
B. Miss France of 1954
C. daughter of W. C. Fields

8 Give the full name of the restaurant's young parking attendant, Kookie.

9 What did Kookie want to do instead of parking cars?

13 According to the theme song, which of the following would you not meet at 77 Sunset Strip?
A. highbrows
B. hipsters
C. gypsters
D. phoney tipsters

16 What did that title refer to?

17 Name the million-selling hit record tie-in to 77 Sunset Strip; it was released in 1959 by Edd Byrnes and Connie Stevens.

The inhabitants of *77 Sunset Strip* size up the situation (above) before moving in on the suspect (right).

18 What inspired the song?

19 At the time, Connie Stevens also starred in another Warner Bros. detective series. What was it?

20 In 1967 Roger Smith married a dynamic actress/singer. Name her.

21 Match the following characters with their *77 Sunset Strip*-cloned series:

A. Cricket Blake
B. Melody Mercer
C. Cha-Cha O'Brien

1. *Bourbon Street Beat*
2. *Hawaiian Eye*
3. *Surfside Six*

22 *77 Sunset Strip* was completely revamped for its final season. Who was the only regular retained on the show?

23 A few years after *77 Sunset Strip* was cancelled, Efrem Zimbalist, Jr. was back in another law enforcement series. What was it?

24 In the 1980s, the daughter of Efrem Zimbalist, Jr. plays one half of another suave and witty detective team. Name the actress and the program.

25 Like Edd Byrnes, Roger Smith released an album designed to build on the success of *77 Sunset Strip*. What was the album called?

THE NIGHT STALKER   (1974-75)

20 What was the name of the murderous ancient Indian sorcerer played by Richard Kiel?

1 By profession Carl Kolchak (Darren McGavin) was a _____.

2 For what firm did he work?

3 Who was his boss?

4 What made Kolchak's murder investigations so unusual?

5 What were the police always doing to his evidence?

6 What was the name of the first of the two TV movies that spawned the series?

7 What creature did Kolchak encounter in it?

8 In what city did that story take place?

9 What was the title of the second TV movie?

10 Where did that story take place?

11 What was the villain this second time out?

12 In what city was Kolchak once a big-shot reporter?

13 Where was his firm based during the series?

14 Long before *The Night Stalker*, Kolchak had a very similar starring role. What was it?

15 Who were Ron Updyke and Monique Marmelstein?

16 Who was Emily Cowles?

17 Where did Kolchak uncover a werewolf?

18 What was the profession of Robert Palmer (played by Tom Skerritt), the man who sold his soul to the Devil?

19 In another series, the actor who played Kolchak's boss played boss to a TV cop whose character was based on a real-life detective. What was that series?

21 What happened when construction workers dug up prehistoric eggs from their underground nest?

22 What particular victims did a pyromaniacal ghost seek out?

23 How did Catherine Rawlins become a vampire?

24 Who was Mr. R.I.N.G.?

25 What ratings distinction can the original TV movie claim?

26 Kolchak uncovered a mythical legendary heroine sacrificing youg men in exchange for immortality. Who was she?

1 As the credits flashed on the screen at the beginning of each episode of *The Rockford Files*, what could be heard in the background?

A. the theme song
B. Rockford's voice
C. Rockford's answering machine
D. police sirens

2 What did Jim Rockford use as a combination home and office?

3 Where was it located?

4 The theme from *The Rockford Files* was a pop hit in 1975. Name the artist who released it.

5 Why did Rockford have so many friends who were ex-cons?

6 Who was Angel Martin?

7 Who played Angel?

8 Who was Rocky?

9 What job did Rocky hold before he retired?

10 What was his favorite sport?

11 And his fondest wish?

12 Name Rockford's Los Angeles police contact.

13 Who was Beth Davenport?

14 Rockford's friend, Meg Dougherty, was handicapped. How?

15 Who played investigator Lance White, Rockford's friendly competitor?

16 What other detective role did that actor play after *The Rockford Files* ended?

17 In a crossover plot to help launch a new series, Rockford teamed up with a young sleuth. Name the sleuth and the series.

18 Who played the title character?

19 In one episode of *The Rockford Files*, "that lady from the camera commercials" was a special guest. Name her.

20 What camera commercials had she made?

21 James Garner did a western series a few years before *The Rockford Files*, and another right after it. What were they?

22 When *The Rockford Files* first went into syndication, what was it called?

Two performers known for a different type of "commercial" partnership team up in an episode of *The Rockford Files*.

1 Which of the following was *not* part of the first season *NBC Mystery Movie* line-up?
 A. *Cannon*
 B. *Columbo*
 C. *McCloud*
 D. *McMillan and Wife*

2 In what city was *McMillan and Wife* set?

3 What did Rock Hudson's character do for a living?

4 Who played his wife, Sally?

5 Who was his chief assistant at the office?

6 Who played Mildred, the McMillans' housekeeper?

7 The same actress also had a role in a TV sitcom at the same time. Name the series, and the role she played.

McCloud (top and top right); *McCoy* (center left); *Madigan* (center right); *Banacek* (lower left).

8 The same actress was *also* plugging paper towels in a TV commercial at the time. What was the brand, and what was her character's name in the commercial?

9 For its final season, *McMillan and Wife* changed to *McMillan*. What happened to Sally?

10 Who played the title role in *McCloud?*

11 During the 1950s and 1960s, that actor had been a major supporting character in a TV western series. Name the series, and the role he played.

14 Was Thomas Banacek's ethnic background:
A. Russian
B. Polish American
C. Eastern European
D. Italian

15 What did he do for a living?

16 In the kickoff episode of *Banacek*, how was the kidnapping of a star football player staged?

17 The Snoop Sisters were undercover police detectives. True or False?

18 In the *Cool Million* segments, what did the title refer to?

20 In the following *Mystery Movie* series, match the title with the performer:
A. *Hec Ramsey*
B. *Lanigan's Rabbi*
C. *McCoy*
D. *The Snoop Sisters*

1. Tony Curtis
2. Helen Hayes
3. Richard Boone
4. Art Carney

21 What *Mystery Movie* series was based on a successful 1968 theatrical film starring Richard Widmark?

22 Who composed the *Mystery Movie* theme?

24 The *Amy Prentiss* segments first played as a special episode of what regular weekly series?
A. *Quincy*
B. *The Rockford Files*
C. *Hill Street Blues*
D. *Ironside*

12 In what city did Sam McCloud operate?

13 Where was *Banacek* set?

19 Which *Mystery Movie* series featured James McEachin as a black detective in Los Angeles?
A. *Farrady and Company*
B. *Tenafly*
C. *Amy Prentiss*
D. *Barnaby Jones*

23 Which of these regular weekly series started under the *Movie Mystery* umbrella?
A. *Quincy*
B. *The Rockford Files*
C. *Hill Street Blues*
D. *Ironside*

Quincy (top right); *McMillan and Wife* (center left and center right); *Lanigan's Rabbi* (lower right).

1 Give the religious name of the flying nun.

2 What was her name before she became a nun?

3 Who played her?

4 Who influenced the girl to become a nun?

5 What relationship existed between that person and the girl herself?

6 Who played that person?

7 Where was the nuns' convent located?

8 What was the name of the convent?

9 The flying nun was very petite; how much did she weigh?

10 What article of clothing assisted her to fly?

11 What was the name of the young playboy and discotheque owner the flying nun was constantly bumping into?

12 Who played this character?

13 Who played the stern Mother Superior?

14 What was the name of the likable police captain?

15 Who played him?

16 Sister Sixto, the Puerto Rican nun, was constantly trying to master a skill. What was it?

17 Who played Sister Sixto?

18 In the last year of the series an orphaned boy was added to the cast. What was his name?

19 What young actor played the orphan?

20 Who played Sister Ana?

21 Upon what book was the TV series based?

22 Who wrote the book?

23 What was the first TV series to star the actress who played the flying nun?

24 What was the name of the actress's stepfather who was also a stunt double for Errol Flynn?

25 For what TV movie did the actress who played the flying nun win an Emmy for Best Actress?

14 Who played Esmeralda, the shy witch?

15 Name the real-life actor who is the father of the actress who played Samantha.

16 What was the name of Samantha's uncle?

17 Who played the bumbling but charming Aunt Clara?

18 How did Samantha perform her magic?

19 The actress who played Samantha also played Samantha's cousin. What was the cousin's name?

20 William Astor produced and directed the series for Screen Gems. Which cast member is he related to?

21 What was the title of the spin-off series?

22 What was Samantha's maiden name?

1 What was the last name of the family featured on TV's *Bewitched*?

2 Name the city and state in which they lived.

3 What was their address?

4 Who played Samantha, the domesticated witch?

5 What was the name of Samantha's advertising executive husband?

6 Who was the first actor to play Samantha's husband?

7 When health problems forced the above-named actor to leave the series in 1969, who replaced him?

8 What company did Samantha's husband work for?

9 Who played his boss, Larry Tate?

10 Name Samantha's mischievous mother?

11 Who played her?

12 What was the name of Samantha's daughter, who was a little witch in her own right?

13 What was the name of Samantha's son?

40   Samantha, the domesticated witch, sometimes surprises even herself (above). Right: Samantha with her mom and mom-in-law.

1 Name the head of the Munster family and his wife.

2 Who played these characters?

3 What was the head of the family's normal blood pressure?

4 How much did he weigh?

5 What was his wife's maiden name?

6 What was the Munsters' address?

7 What were their son's first and middle names?

8 Name their son's doll.

9 Who played Grampa Munster?

10 How old was Grampa?

11 What was the name of the Munsters' niece?

12 Name the two actresses who played her.

13 The second actress named in the answer to question 12 had a famous mother. Identify her.

14 Name the mortuary where the head of the family worked.

15 How old was his wife?

16 What was the name of Grampa's pet bat?

17 Name the 1966 theatrical movie based on the series.

18 Name the 1981 TV movie based on the series.

19 Only three original cast members appeared in that movie. Name them.

20 How tall is the actor who played the head of the Munster family?
A. 6' 3"
B. 6' 4"
C. 6' 7"
D. 7' 0"

21 What one word did Grampa's pet raven utter?

22 What other early '60s cult favorite TV sitcom also starred Fred Gwynne and Al Lewis?

23 What was the Dragula?

24 What is the name of the recent record released by Butch Patrick?

In the Munster family it's the weird people who are ordinary and the ordinary folk who are weird.

THE GHOST AND MRS. MUIR   (1968-70)

15 Who played the original owner of the cottage in the film version?

16 Who played the new owner in the film?

17 Name the book the leading character "ghost" wrote in the movie version?

18 Who was credited as author?

19 Who published it?

20 This was the second TV series for the actress who played Mrs. Muir. True or False?

21 In both the movie and the TV series, the family included the same number of children. True or False?

22 What type of dog did the family have?

23 From what city did Mrs. Muir hail?

24 Jonathan can also see Captain Gregg. True or False?

25 Who first saw the ghost?

1 Name the original owner/occupant of the haunted cottage.

2 Who played him in the series?

3 Where was the cottage located, and what was it called?

4 Name the owner's nephew, the realtor who sold the home.

5 Who played that character?

6 To whom did he sell the cottage?

7 Why did the new owner buy the cottage?

8 Who played the new owner?

9 The new owner had two children; name them and give their ages.

10 Who played the children?

11 What was the new owner's occupation?

12 Name the family's dog.

13 Give the name of the housekeeper and the actress who played her.

14 The TV series was based on a movie. Give its title and date of release.

26 A cast member on the TV series appeared in TV commercials for toothpaste at the age of four. Who was it?

An interesting portrait of the cast of *The Ghost and Mrs. Muir*. Being a ghost, one of them shouldn't be there.

MORK AND MINDY (1978-82)

1 *Mork and Mindy* was a spin-off of what other series?

2 What was Mindy's last name?

3 Name Mork's home planet, and his superior there.

4 Who provided the voice for Mork's superior?

5 In what city and state is *Mork and Mindy* set?

6 What was the address of Mindy's apartment house?

7 Who played Frederick, Mindy's father?

8 What type of store did Frederick own?

9 Why was Mork sent to Earth as a punishment?

10 What is Mindy's telephone number?

11 Who played the very strange Exidor?

12 What was the name of the delicatessen run by Remo DaVinci?

13 Who played Remo, and who played his sister Jean?

14 What is the expression for "good-bye" on Mork's home planet?

15 What shape was the spacecraft in which Mork came to Earth?

16 Name Mork and Mindy's son, and the performer who played him.

17 What was so unusual about the birth of their son?

18 What is the distance from Earth to the planet Ork?

19 What is Mork's favorite TV series?

20 Who played Mindy's neighbor Franklin Bickley?

21 What did Mork do at the end of each episode?

22 Who played Mindy's "swinging" grandmother?

23 What was the grandmother's name?

24 A little boy patronized the music store owned by Mindy's father. Name him.

25 Who played that character?

26 What did Mr. Bickley do for a living?

27 Give the English word for the Orkon word "Shazbat."

28 What was Mindy's occupation during the 1980-81 season?

29 What role did Foster Brooks play during that season?

When alien Mork moves in, Mindy's never sure what's going to happen next.

KID STUFF—
SATURDAY MORNING HEROES

1 Where was Superman raised?

2 What is Superman's costume made from?

3 Who originally conceived of Superman?

4 In what film did George Reeves make his debut?

5 What member of the TV cast appeared in the 1978 movie, *Superman*, in an unbilled cameo role?

6 What was Inspector Henderson's first name?

7 Name Superman's home planet.

8 What part did Robert Shayne play?

9 Where did Clark Kent most often change into his Superman outfit?

10 Clark Kent lived at the Standish Arms. True or False?

Two actresses played Lois Lane in *The Adventures of Superman* and they're both pictured here.

11 The title of the first episode was:
   A. "The Story of Superman"
   B. "Superman on Earth"
   C. "Superman Arrives"

12 Why was one episode titled "The Wedding of Superman"?

13 Superman's X-ray vision cannot penetrate what substance?

14 Finish this line: "A never-ending battle for _____, _____, and the _____ _____."

15 For what newspaper did Clark Kent work?

16 Which member of the cast committed suicide?

17 Comic book character Lex Luthor was never mentioned on the series. True or False?

18 Complete this line: "It's a bird! It's a _____! It's _____!"

Phyllis Coates is seen above; Noel Neill, who took over the role, appears in the small color picture with Superman.

THE LONE RANGER   (1949-57)

5 Who played the Lone Ranger for almost 200 episodes?

6 Who played the Lone Ranger for only one season?

10 What were the Lone Ranger's bullets made of?

11 Where did that material come from?

12 What was the name of Tonto's horse?

13 What was the name of the Lone Ranger's horse?

14 What was the name of the Lone Ranger's nephew?

15 What was the name of his nephew's horse?

16 What was the Lone Ranger's mask made from?

17 The Lone Ranger always shot to kill. True or False?

18 Kemo sabe's meaning has been variously given as "trusty scout" and "faithful friend." True or False?

19 In what state did the Rangers operate?

20 On what network was the series aired?

21 The creators of *The Lone Ranger* also created another show. Name it.

22 *The Lone Ranger* began on radio more than 16 years before it came to television. True or False?

23 Don Reid, Jr.'s son became a '60s crime fighter. Name him.

1 What musical piece was used as a theme for *The Lone Ranger*?

2 What was the true identity of the Lone Ranger?

3 He was the only survivor of an ambush by whose gang?

4 Who played the gang leader?

7 Name the Lone Ranger's brother.

8 Who was Tonto?

9 Who played Tonto?

24 What did the following have in common:
A. Don Pedro O'Sullivan
B. José the Bandit
C. "Professor" Horatio Tucker

THE ADVENTURES OF ROBIN HOOD   (1955-58)

1 Who starred as Robin Hood?

2 In what century were the stories set?

3 Who did Robin and his Merry Men steal from, and what did they do with their spoils?

4 Complete this line from the theme song, "_____ by the bad, _____ by the good."

5 On what network was the series broadcast?

6 Two actors played Little John; name them.

7 Little John's real name was John Little. True or False?

8 What location did Robin and his Merry Men call home?

9 What was the syndicated title of *The Adventures of Robin Hood*?

10 Two actresses played Maid Marian. Name them.

11 What was Maid Marian's last name?

12 What was Robin Hood's full title?

13 Who played Will Scarlett?

14 Who played the sheriff?

15 What city was the sheriff's domain?

16 The show's star was born in:
A. Scotland
B. England
C. Ireland
D. the United States

17 What was King Richard's nickname?

18 Who was his brother?

19 Where had King Richard gone?

20 Friar Tuck was played by Alexander Gauge. True or False?

21 An updated cartoon version of *Robin Hood* was aired in 1967. What was it called?

22 In that story, what location took the place of Sherwood Forest?

Robin Hood sets his sights on any super hero's prime target—justice for all.

THE ROY ROGERS SHOW   (1951-57)

1 What was the name of Roy's ranch?

2 What kind of dog did he have, and what was the dog's name?

3 Who played Pat Brady?

4 What was the name of Pat's jeep?

5 What was Pat's middle name?

6 What was the name of Roy's horse?

7 After the horse died, Roy Rogers:
   A. erected a memorial to the animal
   B. had the horse stuffed
   C. passed on the name to another horse

8 How was Roy Rogers billed on the show?

9 What was the name of Dale Evans' horse?

10 How was Dale Evans billed on the show?

11 What song did they sing at the end of each episode?

12 On what network was the series broadcast?

13 What is Roy Rogers' real name?

14 What is Dale Evans' real name?

15 What was Roy's dog called in the credits?

16 Roy's horse was a Palomino. True or False?

17 What singing group was often featured on the show?

18 How many guns did Roy wear?

19 How many guns did Dale wear?

20 What town was near Roy's ranch?

Two vintage studies of the daddy of all the cowboys, Roy Rogers.

Captain Video (left) and the Ranger (right), on the alert for alien and destructive forces. 53

TRIVIA ROUNDUP

1 Name the famous film star who introduced the first episode of *Gunsmoke*.

2 What was the real name of the cockatoo that played Fred on *Baretta*?

5 On *Gilligan's Island*, Ginger Grant changed her original last name because it would not fit on a theater marquee. What was it?

7 What was the middle name of Sgt. Philip Esterhaus on *Hill Street Blues*?

9 On *Bonanza*, what was Hoss Cartwright's real first name?

10 Who played Fred Johnson, the one-armed man, on *The Fugitive*?

3 On *Leave It to Beaver*, June Cleaver was from East St. Louis, Illinois. True or False?

4 What was Buddy Sorrell's real first name on *The Dick Van Dyke Show*?

6 *Combat*'s Sgt. Chip Saunders was from Chicago. What did he do before the war?

8 When did Bob and Emily Hartley celebrate their wedding anniversary?
A. June 10
B. April 15
C. September 9

11 Name both of the actors who played Lt. Col. Donald Penobscott on *M*A*S*H*.

12 Who played Mary Richards' parents on *The Mary Tyler Moore Show*?

13 On *Barney Miller*, the original title of Det. Ron Harris's book *Blood on the Badge* was:
A. *Precinct Diary*
B. *A Cop's Life*
C. *The Streets*

15 What was the full name of the Cleveland girl that Max Klinger of *M*A*S*H* married and later divorced?

17 What was Jim Rockford's middle name?

18 Who was the first mystery guest on *What's My Line*?

21 Which Barkley brother was written out of the show after the first season of *The Big Valley*?

22 Who was the first guest to sign Carol Burnett's guest book?

14 Bartholomew was the middle name of what regular character on *The Adventures of Superman*?

16 On one episode Quincy's first initial was revealed. Was it:
A. J
B. S
C. R
D. P

19 Name both actresses who played Sam on *Richard Diamond, Private Detective*.

20 What was Granny's full name on *The Beverly Hillbillies*?

23 Who provided the voice of John Beresford Tipton on *The Millionaire*?

ANSWERS

Wagon Train

14 Mr. Reston
15 Hal Needham, whose movies include *Hooper*, a story about stuntmen which starred another former stuntman, Burt Reynolds.
16 *Hec Ramsey*
17 Victor De Costa
18 Randolph Scott
19 *Have Tux, Will Travel*
20 True
21 *Medic*
22 A derringer

Maverick

WAGON TRAIN
(Page 4)
1 California
2 Seth Adams
3 Ward Bond
4 Chris Hale
5 John McIntire
6 St. Joseph, Missouri
7 Robert Horton
8 Scott Miller
9 Duke Shannon
10 Charlie Wooster
11 Frank McGrath
12 Kate Crowley
13 Barbara Stanwyck; *The Big Valley* (1965-68).
14 *Wagonmaster*
15 Ben Johnson
16 Mormon leader Elder Wiggs
17 *Major Adams—Trailmaster*
18 ABC
19 James Arness; *Gunsmoke* (1955-73).

20 Ward Bond, who played the wagon master from 1957 to 1960, died in 1960.

HAVE GUN WILL TRAVEL
(Page 6)
1 Richard Boone
2 San Francisco
3 The Hotel Carlton
4 Room 314
5 Mr. McGunnis
6 Olan Soulé
7 "Have Gun—Will Travel, Wire Paladin, San Francisco."
8 "The Ballad of Paladin"
9 Johnny Western
10 Bernard Herrmann
11 Hey Boy and Hey Girl.
12 Kam Tong and Lisa Lu.
13 Colt .45

Have Gun Will Travel

MAVERICK
(Page 7)
1 James Garner
2 Lo Ball
3 He was a gambler.
4 Bart Maverick, played by Jack Kelly.
5 Brent Maverick, played by Robert Colbert.
6 Richard Long
7 A $1000 bill
8 Beauregard
9 Roger Moore
10 Bart
11 April 7, 1847
12 *Bret Maverick*
13 The Red Ox Saloon
14 Ed Bruce
15 *Young Maverick*
16 Ben Maverick
17 Harvard
18 Charles Frank
19 Susan Blanchard

RAWHIDE
(Page 8)
1 1880's
2 Gil Favor, played by Eric Fleming.
3 San Antonio, Texas; Sedalia, Kansas.
4 Ned Washington and Dmitri Tiomkin composed the theme; Frankie Laine sang it.
5 *High Noon*
6 Clint Eastwood
7 Midnight

8 George Washington Wishbone, generally known as Wishbone.
9 Peter Nolan, played by Sheb Wooley.
10 "The Purple People Eater"
11 Jed Colby
12 Eric Fleming
13 Eric Fleming drowned while filming *High Jungle*.
14 3000 head of cattle
15 Lionhead
16 **A-2** (Robert Cabal—Hey Soos); **B-4** (James Murdock—Mushy); **C-5** (Charles Gray—Clay Forrester); **D-6** (Rock Shahan—Joe Scarlett); **E-1** (Steve Raines—Jim Quince); **F-3** (David Watson—Ian Cabot).
17 True
18 Raymond St. Jacques
19 St. Jacques was the first black actor to be featured in a regular western series.
20 Chuck Wagon dog food
21 "Spaghetti" westerns

THE WILD, WILD WEST
(Page 10)
1 James T. West

The Wild, Wild West

The Rifleman

2 Major
3 Robert Conrad
4 Ulysses S. Grant
5 James Gregory (in the first episode) and Roy Engle.
6 Artemus Gordon
7 Ross Martin
8 Charles Aidman
9 Jeremy Pike
10 *Mr. Lucky*
11 Dr. Miguelito Loveless
12 Michael Dunn
13 Duke and Cacao.
14 Five
15 Orrin Cobb
16 Richard Kiel
17 Nimrod
18 *The Wild, Wild West Revisited*
19 Red West
20 True

THE RIFLEMAN
(Page 11)
1 Lucas McCain, played by Chuck Connors.
2 Mark, played by Johnny Crawford.
3 Blue Boy
4 North Fork
5 New Mexico
6 The Last Chance Saloon
7 Bill Quinn
8 Ellen

9 A modified .44 Winchester
10 12 shots
11 Micah Torrance
12 Paul Fix
13 Carroll O'Connor
14 Joe Higgins
15 *Dick Powell's Zane Grey Theater*
16 Millie Scott
17 The Old Dunlop Ranch
18 "Cindy's Birthday"
19 *Branded*
20 Bobbie Crawford, Jr.
21 *Laramie*
22 Andy Sherman
23 Chuck Connors played baseball and basketball.

DOCTOR WHO
(Page 12)
1 From the planet Gallifrey. As one of the race of Time Lords on the planet, he knows the secrets of time and space travel and uses a vehicle known as the TARDIS to carry him throughout the universe.
2 "Time and Relative Dimensions in Space"
3 It looks like a London police phone booth. The chameleon circuit (which allows the TARDIS to assume any shape

appropriate to its environment) broke while it was in that form. Over several hundred years the Doctor has never gotten around to fixing it.
4 He is over 750 years old.
5 William Hartnell (The First Doctor); Patrick Troughton (The Second Doctor); Jon Pertwee (The Third Doctor); Tom Baker (The Fourth Doctor); Peter Davison (The Fifth Doctor); and Colin Baker (The Sixth Doctor). (Colin and Tom Baker are not related.) Note that Richard Hurndall played The First Doctor in *The Five Doctors* special in 1979.
6 Each of the performers is presented as a new "regeneration" of the Doctor. Thus you're meeting the same person but in a different body.
7 Twelve; he is currently on his fifth regeneration.
8 **A.** The Fifth Doctor (Peter Davison); **B.** The Second Doctor (Patrick Troughton); **C.** The Third Doctor (Jon Pertwee); **D.** The Fourth Doctor (Tom Baker).
9 A renegade Time Lord

Doctor Who

dedicated to evil and to the destruction of the Doctor.
10 Roger Delgado (who died in 1973) and Anthony Ainley.
11 **A.** Tegan Jovanka (Janet Fielding); **B.** Liz Shaw (Caroline John); **C.** Leela (Louise Jameson); **D.** Sara Jane Smith (Elisabeth Sladen).
12 "Reverse the *polarity* of the *neutron flow*." This was one of the Third Doctor's favorite "explanations" of how he achieved some scientific miracle.
13 **B.** The Ewoks were the pint-sized allies of Luke Skywalker in the feature film *Return of the Jedi*.
14 "Exterminate!"
15 Davros, an evil scientist on the planet Skaro.
16 Gold; it blocked off their circulation systems.
17 **A.** Sixth (and the Fifth for two stories); **B.** First; **C.** Third; **D.** Second; **E.** Fourth; **F.** Fifth.
18 Romana. Actress Mary Tamm left after six stories and was replaced by Lalla Ward.
19 1. a rock made of the mineral Jethrik; 2. the planet Calufrax;

ANSWERS

3. a pendant made of the Great Seal of the planet Diplos; **4.** a statue; **5.** a relic swallowed by a giant squid-like creature; **6.** the Princess Astra of Atrios (Lalla Ward).

20 A dog-like mobile computer. He was introduced in the story "The Invisible Enemy," when he left the man who built him (Professor Marius) in order to travel with the Doctor. Later, the Doctor himself built two other K-9 models.

21 An international military force set up to deal with extraterrestrial threats to Earth. The name was an acronym for United Nations Intelligence Task Force.

22 Brigadier Alistair Lethbridge-Stewart, played by Nicholas Courtney, who had first suggested forming such a force after successfully battling an attempted invasion of the Earth with the Doctor.

23 William Hartnell and Tom Baker. William Hartnell died in 1975, so Richard Hurndall played the character of the First Doctor in the special. However, Hartnell was seen at the very beginning of the show in a film clip taken from a 1964 episode. Tom Baker was unavailable for the special, so his character appeared briefly in footage from a 1979 story ("Shada") that had never been aired.

24 Sarah Jane Smith, when she was controlled by the force in the fossilized hand of an alien criminal, Eldrad, in the episode, "The Hand of Fear." For years after the episode first aired Elisabeth Sladen, the actress who played Sarah Jane Smith, was begged by fans to repeat the famous line.

25 False. He is known simply as the Doctor. *Doctor Who* is just the title of the series—and the question posed by some people upon first meeting him. "Doctor? Doctor Who?"

26 A character in "Arc of Infinity" played by future|Sixth Doctor Colin Baker. Maxil was a commander of the guards on Gallifrey. Ironically, Maxil was ordered to hunt and execute the Fifth Doctor.

27 Peter Cushing, in *Doctor Who and the Daleks* (1965) and *Daleks—Invasion Earth 2150 A.D.* (1966).

28 The sonic screwdriver

ALL MY CHILDREN
(Page 14)

1 Erica Kane Martin Brent Cudahy Chandler—so far.

All My Children

2 Jason Maxwell was accidentally shot by Mona Kane.
3 **B.** The Glamorama
4 True
5 **D.** She was killed while skiing; Tony sabotaged her skis.
6 Tad, who revealed Silver's involvement to the police.
7 **C.** *Citizen Kane;* Warrick played Kane's first wife.
8 To marry a banker.
9 True
10 **A-4** (Sam—plumber/electrician); **B-3** (Mark—pianist); **C-2** (Donna—singer); **D-1** (Marian—realtor).
11 Cliff
12 Jenny, Opal's daughter.
13 Chuck
14 **A.** Phoebe
15 Gwen Verdon

All My Children

16 Plastic surgery; the actress's face lift was written into the script as surgery to repair disfigurement caused to Margo in a fire.
17 The storyline stated that Erica had suffered a mental blackout and believed she had had a miscarriage.
18 Nina
19 False. Mary Fickett (Ruth); Ray MacDonnell (Joe); and Susan Lucci (Erica) have all been with the daytime drama since its inception.
20 Cocaine
21 **B.** a former Nazi
22 *One Life to Live* aired on June 15, 1968; *All My Children* was first seen on January 5, 1970.
23 The Boutique
24 TV talk show host Dick Cavett

THE EDGE OF NIGHT
(Page 16)

1 WMON
2 WEON
3 **A-3** (Larry Hagman—Ed Gibson); **B-4** (Tony Roberts—

The Edge of Night

Lee Pollock); **C-1** (Martin Sheen—Roy Sanders); **D-2** (Frank Gorshin—Smiley Wilson).
4 Stephanie Martin
5 The Video Disco
6 False; he was a tough guy with a heart of gold.
7 Star Wilson
8 Children of the Earth
9 Jefferson Brown; he had had his face reconstructed to look like Sky, his employer, so that he could assume Sky's fortune.
10 Gunther's evil twin brother.
11 With poisoned makeup.
12 *The Mansion of the Damned*
13 Collin and Keith.
14 Jamie
15 For a million-dollar fee, they received new faces through plastic surgery.
16 **C**—Kevin; **B**—Logan; **D**—Eliot; **E**—Jefferson; **A**—Sky.
17 Gunther; Sky, angered by Gavin's romantic interest in Martine, ordered Gunther to ruin Gavin's career.
18 False; Cliff unhappily left his sweetheart for an important job in Washington, D.C.
19 She was a writer for many years.
20 They became private investigators.
21 He was actually Keith Whitney, Geraldine's schizophrenic son.
22 Blind, but she eventually regained her eyesight.
23 True; she felt she was losing her husband Miles' affection to Nicole. The plot didn't work.
24 The Unicorn

DAYS OF OUR LIVES
(Page 17)

1 Shenanigans
2 Chris and Danny.
3 **A-4** (Tom Horton—Alice); **B-2** (Doug Williams—Julie); **C-1** (Roman Brady—Marlena); **D-3** (Mickey Horton—Maggie).

ANSWERS

Days of Our Lives

23 The death of their son D.J.
24 He fell off a cliff during a struggle with the evil Stefano.
25 He drives a motorcycle.
26 Stefano had faked his own death and "returned," so he chose as his symbol the mythical bird, the phoenix, which was believed to rise from its own ashes.

The Young and the Restless

4 He wanted to use her money to pay off his gambling debts.
5 Blondie's
6 University Hospital
7 Leukemia
8 False; Roman stopped her romantic advances before she could take him to bed.
9 A raven's feather
10 Andre Di Mera; Jake Kositchek was the Salem Strangler.
11 True
12 True
13 Wife-beating
14 Angel
15 Bill Hayes, who also played Doug.
16 An hourglass
17 MacDonald Carey, playing Tom Horton.
18 False; rock lyricists Tommy Boyce and Bobby Hart write many of the songs.
19 D. All three actors have played the role.
20 Kate Winograd and Linda Anderson.
21 Madame X
22 True; and before she became a nun, Marie was a drug addict.

Days of Our Lives

THE YOUNG AND THE RESTLESS
(Page 18)

1 Genoa City, Wisconsin
2 Sleazy's Bar
3 As head writer for NBC's *Days of Our Lives.*
4 The talented actress and her character Kay had a face lift with the cameras moving into the actual operating room to show the incisions. (See pictures on page 18.)
5 True; trying to lose weight, Traci turned to the school pusher for some "weight-reducing pills."
6 A-2 (Paul Williams—private detective); B-4 (Ashley Abbott—president of Jabot Cosmetics); C-3 (Danny Romalotti—rock singer); D-1 (Julia Newman—model).
7 She was a stripper.
8 Phillip Chancellor
9 He faked his own death.
10 She joined a convent.
11 Gina's
12 He had tried to rape her.
13 Jerry "Cash" Cashman
14 Victor
15 Eric
16 She filed a sex discrimination lawsuit.
17 True
18 Hairdresser
19 Teen model Cricket
20 He used makeup and a toupee to disguise himself as a white businessman. (See pictures on page 18.)

General Hospital

21 Elwood—played by Jon St. Elwood.
22 Traci
23 Brad, a neurosurgeon, left medicine when his fiancee's son died under his scalpel.
24 Laura Lee, daughter of Bill Bell, who created *The Young and the Restless.*
25 A veil

GENERAL HOSPITAL
(Page 20)

1 Milton Berle, making his first appearance on a soap.
2 The actress was 14.
3 True
4 A hit-and-run driver
5 Ed Platt
6 True
7 True, and the actress sent most of them on to the FBI.
8 He was cast as the rapist and played the role for months.
9 True; it scored a remarkable 52 percent share of the audience and even outdid the wedding of Prince Charles and Lady Di.
10 Ginny Blake, who was about to be blackmailed by Brock.
11 Elizabeth Taylor
12 To a farm in upstate New York.
13 Audrey told Tom that Steve was the baby's father; she had divorced Tom and wanted to marry Steve, so she couldn't reveal that she had Tom's son.
14 Luke and Robert turned Mikos' own freezing machine on him and froze him to death.
15 The Haunted Star
16 The worldwide evil spy organization DVX.
17 A-3 (John Beradino—Dr. Steve Hardy); B-2 (Roy Thinnes—Dr. Phil Brewer); C-4 (James Sikking—Dr. Jim Hobart); D-1 (Sammy Davis, Jr.—Eddie Phillips).
18 B. She pretended she was blind; the ruse backfired when he discovered the truth.
19 D. Kelly's
20 Lassa fever
21 Her father was dying in China and she rushed back to be with him.
22 A powerful new energy source known as "the Prometheus disc."
23 Malkuth

ANSWERS

The Secret Storm

THE SECRET STORM
(Page 22)

1 Woodbridge
2 Sad; wife and mother Ellen Ames died from the injuries she received in a car accident.
3 He tried to kill the man who caused his mother's accident.
4 Georgina, the previous owner.
5 He had killed Georgina and her children.
6 He fell through a large standing mirror after seeing a vision of Georgina.
7 False. He did marry her, but he finally returned to the church.
8 History
9 Piano
10 Golf
11 False; she married Kip before Lisa was born.
12 On a deserted island.
13 Nina; daughter of his high-school Spanish teacher.
14 Woodbridge University
15 Accidentally, in a boating mishap.
16 Governor
17 No; his drug dealing was discovered and he was sent to prison.
18 True
19 Robert Landers
20 Ellen, Myra, and Valerie.
21 He suffered a heart attack.
22 A gunshot wound inflicted by one of his father's mobster friends.
23 Yes, in a tearful scene with Amy, Valerie, and Lisa.
24 She left to pursue a singing career.

DARK SHADOWS
(Page 23)

1 Dr. Julia Hoffman
2 Collinsport, Maine
3 Newport, Rhode Island
4 Louis Edmonds, who also plays Langley on *All My Children*.
5 Three: Professor Eliot Stokes; Count Petofi; and Mordecai Grimes.
6 True; she played Daphne Harridge.
7 He was a 200-year-old vampire.
8 True
9 **A.** He claimed it came to him

Dragnet

during a dream.
10 True
11 Custom-designed vampire fangs, for which ABC paid $200.
12 **C.** cousin
13 None; she had never even watched a soap before being cast in *Dark Shadows*.
14 **D.** He played all three roles.
15 Jonathan
16 Donna McKechnie
17 False; the novelty wore off after a couple of weeks and the show was dropped.
18 He wanted to marry Maggie Evans; if he married her while he was still a vampire, he would inevitably turn her into one as well.
19 *House of Dark Shadows* (1970) and *Night of Dark Shadows* (1971).
20 He continually forgot his lines and used those uncomfortable moments to try out entertaining facial expressions until he remembered what to say.
21 To take care of young David Collins.
22 Adam and Eve.
23 He was a Shakespearean actor.

TALK SHOW TRIVIA
(Page 24)

1 Arthur Treacher
2 True
3 Cleveland
4 Victoria May Budinger
5 **B.** Regis Philbin

The Steve Allen Show

6 **A.** 1972
7 Carl
8 False; he used to be a Marine.
9 "This Could Be the Start of Something Big"
10 The Great Carsoni
11 Lyle
12 Tom Poston
13 True
14 **B.** 1957
15 **C.** Marines
16 Gene Rayburn
17 Jack Paar
18 Joan Rivers
19 Iowa
20 *Who Do You Trust?*
21 José Melis
22 Paul Anka
23 Dick Cavett
24 True

DRAGNET
(Page 28)

1 Los Angeles, which also provided the setting for the series.
2 Joe Friday, played by Jack Webb.
3 Sergeant
4 Officer Frank Smith
5 Ben Alexander played the role from 1953 to 1959.
6 "Just the facts, ma'am."
7 Joe Friday's badge number. The show also went into syndication under the name *Badge 714*.
8 True
9 *Protect* the *innocent*.
10 False; he did not write the stories, though his distinctive style obviously set the tone for those who did.
11 Mark VII
12 The logo was chiseled in stone. Viewers saw a burly arm hit a die marker twice.
13 Officer Bill Gannon
14 Harry Morgan
15 The year was added, making the title *Dragnet '67*.
16 *Gangbusters*
17 Ray Anthony and his orchestra.
18 Stan Freberg
19 *The Tonight Show*; Webb performed the skit with Johnny Carson, who concluded that if he ever caught Claude Cooper—he'd clobber him!
20 True, of course.
21 Yes, in 1959 Sgt. Friday was promoted to lieutenant and Officer Smith was promoted to sergeant.
22 The results of the trial for each

apprehended suspect, including the length of any jail sentences imposed.

23 *Adam-12*

PERRY MASON
(Page 30)

1 Lawyer and novelist Erle Stanley Gardner

2 Raymond Burr

3 **B.** Generally, the murder took place halfway into the one-hour show. The other half would focus on the trial.

4 True

5 Paul Drake, who operated his own private investigation agency.

6 William Hopper

7 District Attorney Hamilton Burger

8 William Talman

9 Della Street

10 Barbara Hale

11 Mason's switchboard operator and receptionist.

12 Lieutenant Arthur Tragg, played by Raymond Collins.

13 Hamilton Burger

14 False; even when he took vacation trips, he inevitably got involved in a murder.

15 False—sort of. In "The Case of the Deadly Verdict," the jury returned a guilty verdict, but Mason won on appeal.

16 **B.** Robert Redford

17 **B.** The cast included a number of the production people who had worked on the series over the years.

18 Erle Stanley Gardner, who created the character of Perry Mason.

19 *The New Adventures of Perry Mason*

20 Monte Markham

21 **D.** The new series lasted barely four months.

22 **C.** *The Edge of Night*

Columbo

COLUMBO
(Page 31)

1 Los Angeles

2 Lieutenant in the homicide division.

3 His first name was never revealed. For all practical purposes, "Lieutenant" served as his first name.

4 A rumpled trench coat

5 Cheap cigars

6 Columbo played by Peter

77 Sunset Strip

Falk), the lead character, did not appear at the start of the episode. He only entered the story when the murder investigation began.

7 At the very beginning of each story viewers saw the guest star commit the murder.

8 *Prescription: Murder*

9 **B.** Rock Hudson. He was starring at the time in *McMillan and Wife*.

10 False; a number of performers appeared several times, playing a different killer on each outing. Jack Cassidy, for instance, played three different killers—two of them in the series' first season.

11 *The Trials of O'Brien* (1965)

12 **A-2** (Ross Martin—rare paintings); **B-1** (Ricardo Montalban—bullfighting); **C-4** (Donald Pleasence—rare wines); **D-3** (Dick Van Dyke—photography).

13 *The NBC Mystery Movie*

14 **A.** a forlorn basset hound. Baretta had a pet cockatoo; Honey West had an ocelot.

15 True; though he referred to her constantly, she was never seen on the screen.

16 Kate Mulgrew; she had played Mary Ryan.

17 The show premiered under the title *Mrs. Columbo*; then the title was changed to *Kate Loves a Mystery*. References to Columbo were dropped, and the lead character even got a new last name—Callahan.

18 CBS, as part of *The CBS Late Movie*.

19 **A.** a mystery writer

20 True; the *Columbo* legend has it that the budget for the star's wardrobe was one of the lowest in TV history.

77 SUNSET STRIP
(Page 32)

1 Private investigators Stuart Bailey and Jeff Spencer.

2 Efrem Zimbalist, Jr. played Bailey; Roger Smith played Spencer.

3 True; Bailey even held an Ivy League Ph.D.

4 Suzanne Fabray

5 **B.** Miss France of 1954

6 **C.** Horse racing

7 **B.** Dino's

8 Gerald Lloyd Kookson, III, played by Edd Byrnes.

9 He wanted to work as a private investigator.

10 Yes, at first he just helped Bailey and Spencer out. By the fourth season, he had become a partner private eye.

11 J.R. Hale, played by Robert Logan.

12 The rhythmic finger clicks

13 **C.** gypsters

14 True

15 *Surfside Six*

16 The location of the Miami Beach houseboat that *those* suave detectives used as their home and office.

17 "Kookie, Kookie, Lend Me Your Comb"

18 Kookie's habit of combing his

hair all the time.

19 *Hawaiian Eye*; she played Cricket Blake.

20 Ann-Margret

21 **A-2** (Cricket Blake, played by Connie Stevens, in *Hawaiian Eye*); **B-1** (Melody Mercer, played by Arlene Howell, in *Bourbon Street Beat*); **C-3** (Cha-Cha O'Brien, played by Margarita Sierra, in *Surfside Six*).

22 Efrem Zimbalist, Jr. as Stuart Bailey.

23 *The F.B.I.*

24 Stephanie Zimbalist; *Remington Steele*.

25 "Beach Romance"

THE NIGHT STALKER
(Page 34)

1 Journalist

2 The Independent News Service

3 Tony Vincenzo, played by Simon Oakland.

4 The murders were frequently perpetrated by nonhuman killers—such as vampires, werewolves, or monsters.

5 Illegally seizing and destroying it.

6 *The Night Stalker*

7 Vampire Janos Skorzeny, played by Barry Atwater.

8 Las Vegas

9 *The Night Strangler*

10 Seattle

11 A murderous, Dorian Gray-like alchemist, played by Richard Anderson.

ANSWERS

The Night Stalker

12 New York City
13 Chicago
14 Casey, the title role in the 1951-52 CBS series *Crime Photographer*; he replaced Richard Carlyle in the role.
15 They were other INS reporters; the roles were played by Jack Grimmage and Carol Ann Susi.
16 Emily Cowles, played by Ruth McDevitt, wrote the "agony" column for the news service.
17 On a luxury liner's final voyage.
18 A politician
19 *Toma*; the title role was based on real-life detective David Toma, and Simon Oakland played his boss, Inspector Spooner.
20 Diablero
21 A reptilian monster began killing them.
22 Associates of a Chicago symphony conductor.
23 Catherine Rawlins (Suzanne Charney) was a victim of the Las Vegas vampire in *The Night Stalker*.
24 An out-of-control military robot.
25 It was the highest-rated TV movie, in terms of audience, up to that time.
26 Helen of Troy, played by Cathy Lee Crosby.

THE ROCKFORD FILES
(Page 35)
1 **C.** Jim Rockford's answering machine, which played his message and then the voice of the caller. There was a new caller for each episode.
2 A house trailer
3 At the Paradise Cove Trailer Colony in Malibu, California.
4 Mike Post, who also co-authored the tune.
5 He had served time for a crime he did not commit.
6 Rockford's former cell mate, a small-time con man released from jail.
7 Stuart Margolin
8 Rockford's dad, played by Noah Beery.
9 He had been a trucker.
10 Fishing
11 He wanted Jim to find a nice girl and get married.
12 Sgt. Dennis Becker, played by Joe Santos.
13 Rockford's attorney friend who bailed him out when his investigations landed him in trouble with the law.
14 She was blind.
15 Tom Selleck
16 Thomas Magnum on *Magnum, P.I.*
17 Richie Brockelman; *Richie Brockelman, Private Eye.*
18 Dennis Dugan
19 Mariette Hartley. Of course, she played a different character.
20 A series of humorous vignettes with James Garner promoting Polaroid cameras and film. The two were so effective together that many viewers assumed they were going together, or even already married.
21 *Nichols*, and a revival of *Maverick* called *Bret Maverick*.
22 *Jim Rockford, Private Investigator*

NBC MYSTERY MOVIE
(Page 36)
1 **A.** *Cannon*; it played on CBS.
2 San Francisco
3 He was the city's police commissioner.
4 Susan St. James
5 Sgt. Charles Enright, played by John Schuck.
6 Nancy Walker
7 *Rhoda*; she played Rhoda's mom.
8 Bounty paper towels; she was known as Rosie.
9 Susan St. James left the series in a contract dispute, so her character was killed off in a plane crash.
10 Dennis Weaver
11 *Gunsmoke*; he played deputy Chester Goode.
12 New York
13 Boston
14 **B.** Polish American
15 He was a private investigator who specialized in collecting rewards from insurance companies for recovering priceless stolen property.
16 He apparently disappeared into thin air under a pile of players; the incident occurred in a packed stadium and before millions of TV viewers.
17 False; they were successful mystery writers who could not resist looking into the real mysteries they ran across.
18 The million dollar fee charged for each case. Of course, results *were* guaranteed.
19 **B.** *Tenafly*; (*Barnaby Jones* played on CBS).
20 **A-3** (*Hec Ramsey*—Richard Boone); **B-4** (*Lanigan's Rabbi*—Art Carney); **C-1** (*McCoy*—Tony Curtis); **D-2** (*The Snoop Sisters*—Helen Hayes).
21 *Madigan*; Widmark appeared in the 1972 TV series as well.
22 Henry Mancini
23 **A.** *Quincy*
24 **D.** *Ironside*

THE FLYING NUN
(Page 38)
1 Sister Bertrille
2 Elsie Ethington
3 Sally Field
4 Sister Jacqueline
5 Sister Jacqueline was the flying nun's aunt.
6 Marge Redmond
7 Near San Juan, Puerto Rico.
8 San Tanco
9 90 lbs.

The Flying Nun

10 The starched cornette that the order wore as part of their habit.
11 Carlos Ramirez
12 Alejandro Rey
13 Madeleine Sherwood
14 Gaspar Formento
15 Vito Scotti
16 The English language
17 Shelley Morrison
18 Marcello
19 Manuel Padilla, Jr.
20 Linda Dangcil
21 *The Fifteenth Pelican*
22 Tere Rios
23 *Gidget*
24 Jock Mahoney
25 *Sybil*

Bewitched

BEWITCHED
(Page 40)
1 Stevens
2 West Port, Connecticut
3 1164 Morning Glory Circle
4 Elizabeth Montgomery
5 Darrin
6 Dick York
7 Dick Sargent
8 McMann and Tate
9 David White
10 Endora
11 Agnes Moorehead
12 Tabitha
13 Adam
14 Alice Ghostley
15 Robert Montgomery
16 Uncle Arthur, played by Paul Lynde.
17 Marion Lorne
18 By wiggling her nose.
19 Serena

20 He is Elizabeth Montgomery's husband.
21 *Tabitha*
22 Dobson

The Munsters

THE MUNSTERS
(Page 41)

1 Herman and Lily.
2 Fred Gwynne and Yvonne De Carlo.
3 −3
4 387 pounds
5 Dracula
6 1313 Mockingbird Lane, Mockingbird Heights
7 Eddie (or Edward) Wolfgang
8 Wolf Wolf
9 Al Lewis
10 350 years old
11 Marilyn
12 Beverly Owen; Pat Priest.
13 Ivy Baker Priest, who was at one time Treasurer of the United States.
14 Gateman, Goodbury, and Graves.
15 157 years old
16 Igor
17 *Munster, Go Home*
18 *The Munsters' Revenge*
19 Fred Gwynne, Yvonne De Carlo, and Al Lewis.
20 **C.** 6'7"
21 "Nevermore"
22 *Car 54, Where Are You?*
23 Grampa's 160-mph coffin car
24 "Whatever Happened to Eddie?"

TOPPER
(Page 42)

1 Cosmo; Leo G. Carroll.
2 The National Security Bank in New York City.
3 Vice president
4 Mr. Shuyler
5 Thurston Hall
6 Henrietta, played by Lee Patrick.
7 George and Marion Kerby.
8 Robert Sterling and Anne

Jeffreys.
9 They were married to each other in real life, as well as on the series.
10 A St. Bernard dog called Neil.
11 The dog drank brandy.
12 Buck
13 The couple were in Europe celebrating their fifth wedding anniversary when they were killed in an avalanche.
14 Katie
15 Kathleen Freeman
16 Margie
17 Edna Skinner
18 Thorne Smith
19 In an automobile accident.
20 Neil the dog
21 "The ghostess with the mostest."
22 "A most sporting spirit."
23 False; she could not see either of them.
24 Kerby
25 Neil the dog

The Ghost and Mrs. Muir

THE GHOST AND MRS. MUIR
(Page 44)

1 Captain Daniel Gregg
2 Edward Mulhare
3 Schooner Bay, New England; Gull Cottage.
4 Claymore Gregg
5 Charles Nelson Reilly
6 Carolyn Muir
7 To find peace and quiet after her divorce.
8 Hope Lange
9 Candy, age eight, and Jonathan, age nine.
10 Kellie Flanagan and Harlan Carraher.
11 She was a free-lance magazine writer.
12 Scruffy
13 Martha, played by Reta Shaw.
14 *The Ghost and Mrs. Muir* (1947)
15 Rex Harrison
16 Gene Tierney

17 *Blood and Swash*
18 Captain X
19 Tacket and Sprogins.
20 False; it was her first TV series.
21 False; there was only one child in the movie but two in the TV series.
22 Fox terrier
23 Philadelphia
24 True
25 Jonathan
26 Kellie Flanagan, who played Mrs. Muir's daughter Candy.

MORK AND MINDY
(Page 45)

1 *Happy Days*
2 McConnell
3 Ork; Orson
4 Ralph James
5 Boulder, Colorado
6 1619 Pine Street
7 Conrad Janis
8 A record store
9 He drew a mustache on the Solar leader.
10 555-1575
11 Robert Donner
12 The New York Deli
13 Jay Thomas; Gina Hecht
14 "Nanu-nanu"
15 Egg-shaped
16 Mearth, played by Jonathan Winters.
17 Mork laid the egg from which their offspring emerged.
18 60 bleems
19 *I Love Lucy*
20 Tom Poston

21 He twisted his ears.
22 Elizabeth Kerr
23 Cora Hudson
24 Eugene
25 Jeffrey Jaquet
26 Mr. Bickley designed greeting cards.
27 "Drat"
28 Mindy worked for a TV station.
29 He played the manager of the TV station.

THE ADVENTURES OF SUPERMAN
(Page 46)

1 In Smallville, U.S.A., by Eben and Sarah Kent.
2 The blankets that wrapped him on his rocket trip to earth as an infant.
3 Two teenagers, writer Jerry Siegel and artist Joe Shuster, in the 1930s.
4 *Gone with the Wind* (1939)
5 Noel Neill
6 Bill (William)
7 Krypton
8 Inspector William Henderson
9 In the storeroom.
10 True
11 **B.** "Superman on Earth"
12 Lois Lane dreamed that she married Superman.
13 Lead
14 "A never-ending battle for truth, justice, and the American way."
15 *The Daily Planet*

Mork and Mindy

ANSWERS

The Adventures of Superman

16 George Reeves
17 True
18 "It's a bird! It's a plane! It's Superman!"

THE LONE RANGER
(Page 48)
1 Rossini's overture to "William Tell"
2 John Reid, a Texas Ranger.
3 Butch Cavendish's Hole in the Wall Gang
4 Glenn Strange
5 Clayton Moore
6 John Hart
7 Dan Reid
8 The Lone Ranger's Indian companion who nursed him back to health after the ambush.
9 Jay Silverheels

The Lone Ranger

64

10 Silver
11 A silver mine that the Lone Ranger and his brother, who later died, discovered together.
12 Scout
13 Silver
14 Dan Reid, Jr.
15 Victor
16 His dead brother's vest.
17 False; he only shot to wound.
18 True
19 Texas
20 ABC
21 *The Green Hornet*
22 True
23 Britt Reid, the Green Hornet.
24 They were all among the Lone Ranger's disguises.

The Adventures of Robin Hood

THE ADVENTURES OF ROBIN HOOD
(Page 49)
1 Richard Greene
2 The 12th century
3 They stole from the rich and gave to the poor.
4 "Feared by the bad, loved by the good."
5 CBS
6 Archie Duncan; Rufus Cruikshank.
7 True
8 Sherwood Forest
9 *Sherwood Forest*
10 Bernadette O'Farrell and Patricia Driscoll.
11 Fitzwater
12 Sir Robin of Locksley
13 Paul Eddington and Will Dearth both played Will Scarlett.
14 Alan Wheatley
15 Nottingham
16 **B.** England
17 Richard the Lion-Hearted
18 Prince John, played by Donald Pleasence.
19 To fight the Crusades.
20 True
21 *Rocket Robin Hood*
22 Sherwood Asteroid

THE ROY ROGERS SHOW
(Page 50)
1 Double R Bar
2 A German shepherd called Bullet.
3 Pat Brady

The Roy Rogers Show

4 Nelliebelle
5 Aloysius
6 Trigger
7 **B.** When Trigger died Roy Rogers had the animal stuffed.
8 "King of the Cowboys"
9 Buttermilk
10 "Queen of the West"
11 "Happy Trails to You"
12 NBC
13 Leonard Slye
14 Frances Octavia Evans
15 Wonder Dog
16 True
17 Sons of the Pioneers
18 Two
19 One
20 Mineral City

Sky King

SKY KING
(Page 52)
1 Schuyler
2 Kirby Grant
3 Penny
4 Gloria Winters
5 **B.** The Songbird
6 Cessna 310-B
7 Clipper
8 Ron Hagerthy
9 False, it was a twin-engined plane.
10 Mitch
11 Grover City
12 Flying Crown Ranch
13 True
14 Nabisco
15 National Biscuit Company
16 **B.** World War II
17 NBC; the show was later rerun on both ABC and CBS.

18 Phoenix
19 Ewing Mitchell
20 Captain Midnight

CAPTAIN VIDEO AND HIS VIDEO RANGERS
(Page 53)
1 Richard Coogan and Al Hodge.
2 Al Hodge
3 DuMont
4 Five times a week.
5 Wagner's Overture to "The Flying Dutchman"
6 The Ranger
7 Don Hastings
8 Dr. Pauli, played by Hal Conklin.
9 True; Al Hodge had played the Green Hornet.
10 Tobor—robot spelled backwards.
11 Galaxy
12 *The Secret Files of Captain Video*
13 **B.** Neutronometer
14 **A.** Guardian of the Safety of the World
15 He was 15.
16 On a mountaintop.
17 Video Rangers

The Mary Tyler Moore Show

TRIVIA ROUNDUP
(Page 54)
1 John Wayne
2 Lala
3 True
4 Maurice
5 Guggenheimer
6 He sold shoes.
7 Freemason
8 **B.** April 15
9 Eric
10 Bill Raisch
11 Beeson Carroll and Mike Henry.
12 Bill Quinn and Nanette Fabray.
13 **A.** *Precinct Diary*
14 Jimmy Olsen
15 LaVerne Esposito
16 **C.** R
17 Scott
18 Phil Rizzuto
19 Mary Tyler Moore and Roxanne Brooks.
20 Daisy Moses
21 Eugene
22 Jim Nabors
23 Paul Frees